The ANOINTING to FINISH

The
ANOINTING
to FINISH

Reaching the Finish Line of
God's Perfect Plan for Your Life

Reginald B. Williams, II

XULON PRESS

Xulon Press
2301 Lucien Way #415
Maitland, FL 32751
407.339.4217
www.xulonpress.com

Printed in the United States of America.

Paperback ISBN-13: 978-1-66281-109-8
Ebook ISBN-13: 978-1-66281-110-4

DEDICATION

How can I say thanks for the things only you have done for me - to God be the Glory. It's my heart's desire to make you proud in every area of my life. You've equipped me with everything pertaining to life and Godliness and it's through you, Lord, I was able to finish. May this manuscript be an encouragement and fresh rhema just like you gave to me to everyone that reads and walk out each principle in Jesus name. I also honor my wife, Asha - my life and ministry partner. You are the epitome of what a true woman of God is, and you are a phenomenal wife, mother, friend, and minister of the gospel. May God grant you every dream and desire; it's an honor to be your Husband. To my awesome kids - Trey and Zoe you are definitely everything a father would dream to have as children. You make your father proud. To my mother Sandra Bowens Williams, you are an awesome mother who taught me that I can do anything I put my hands to do. Thank you for always holding me accountable yet loving me as your only child. I pray this makes you proud. To My Pastors-Lennell and Carol Caldwell – Thank you for being what true pastors are and being an excellent example to your spiritual children. I'm honored to be called a son. To my entire family - Williams, Bowens, Nunn, Berry, Armstrong, Johnsons, Thorntons, Mayhands, Worthy - I want you all to know I am grateful for your prayers, support, and love through the years. I'm so proud of my family. Last, certainly not least my father Rev. Reginald B. Williams, Sr. - I love and miss you dearly. Rest In Peace, and may your legacy of working purposely and consistently continue in my children, and their children's children forever! Thank you for leaving an eternal inheritance in me.

TABLE OF CONTENTS

FOREWORD

By Apostle Lennell D. Caldwell
First Baptist World Changers
International Ministries Detroit, Michigan

HAVE YOU EVER been stuck in life, not able to move to the next or another level? No matter how hard you tried, you didn't move forward. Perhaps you have had the frustration of mundane, mediocrity or even worse, emptiness. You were not able to break through or overcome this experience. Of course, you have! We all have! Life is full of uncertainties, roadblocks, discouragements, pain, or just times of drifting along or just standing still. But there is a solution!

Reginald Williams is on point in this work of God that will change your life. This book," The Anointing to Finish" gives practical and powerful wisdom not only to receive but conceive Gods perfect will and plan for your life. It provides fundamental insight into the power of a dream as an essential element of Gods plan and how God uses it.

This book will engage you into profound, rich and vivid examples of how to overcome obstacles and challenges on life's path of not only conceiving of the plan, the dream but also fulfillment and completion of it. Furthermore, it gives movement to any person's life paralyzed by these obstacles and challenges.

Your faith will stir, and you will be encouraged to get back to God, to try again and keep it moving to see what the end will be and to see the finished product of your dream, your life. You will reinforce your anointing and your power to get it done. You are anointed to do it.

I have revisited the teaching that God has imparted into me and to see it verbalize in my son in the gospel does my heart well. It also does me well seeing that everything that Reginald dreams has come to pass and for him to know that he's anointed to finish.

In a straight forward easy to read way, Reginald Williams reveals the priceless practical, biblical principles for high achievement, personal happiness, and great success. For this reason, I would recommend this book as required reading for every believer. In conclusion, the best way to describe his book and how it contributes to the plans of your life would be by the famous words of a very renowned person, Jesus Christ, "**It is finished.**" So, Live it out!

If God gave you the idea, then it's worth going through the process to finish. He has given you everything you need pertaining to life and Godliness to get you to the finish line. God, for some reason, shows us the end of a thing but never shows us the process. As you read this book my prayer is that you recognize and see the bigger picture and recognize that God really has our best interest at heart.

You see he knew before the foundations of this world that you would finish. Although there will be moments your faith will be tried - keep moving in the direction of what you saw finished. God's way of doing things is far more advanced than ours but with him and through him we can do all things. Your time is not on other people's time. It's out of the realm of time. It's God's perfect timing in your life, and that my friend is all you need. You must recognize your steps are ordered. Reading this book will give you a clear focus of the journey that is needed to complete whatever needs to be finished. You will also be able to reflect after each chapter and take notes on what has become clear to you as God speaks.

There is so much more inside of you. God says I am with you even until the end of the ages your potential is God himself, and he dwells on the inside of you. The enemy wants to stop your momentum, but God wants to empower you to go forward. Don't waddle in the shadows of defeat and death. You have started and now it is time to finish.

Finally, Jesus being the perfect example of finishing, his process to finish was a major challenge, but he endured!

"Therefore, since we are surrounded by so great a cloud of witnesses [who by faith have testified to the truth of God's absolute faithfulness], stripping off every unnecessary weight and the sin which so easily and cleverly entangles us, let us run with endurance and active persistence the race that is set before us, [looking away from all that will distract us and] focusing our eyes on Jesus, who is the Author and Perfecter of faith [the first incentive for our belief and the One who brings our faith to maturity], who for the joy [of accomplishing the goal] set before Him endured the cross, disregarding the shame, and sat down at the right hand of the throne of God [revealing His deity, His authority, and the completion of His work]."

Chapter

1

THE CONCEPTION OF A DREAM

EVERYTHING WE SEE with our natural eyes began somewhere. In fact, a dream can't become a reality unless it is first conceived. Dreams are ordained from God. Dreams are formulated to propel you into your destiny. God's purpose for dreams is to maximize your perception of what you can really do. God has a way of illuminating his thoughts over our thoughts by revealing his thoughts through the scriptures. Jeremiah 29:11 states, "For I know the thoughts I think toward you saith the Lord thoughts of peace and not of evil to give you an expected end." As we began this journey we realized that there are stages of conception.

To understand the process of conception we must understand the biological science of its nature before something is conceived. First, there is a relationship that is started between a male and female. In a relationship there has to be consistency of intimacy between the two in order for conception to take place at an appointed time. Once the seed of a man has been planted inside of a woman, at the appointed time, a purposeful life begins. The nature and personality of God's way of doing things resembles this process.

So, how exactly is a dream conceived? God allows us to first examine the natural before we can comprehend the spiritual. Before conception takes place in the natural there are a number of steps that take place, which makes life itself a miracle performed by God. This is directly parallel to our visions and dreams, when they come to pass in our lives they're totally miraculous to behold, displaying the awesome wonders of our God! Let's walk through these stages of conception together and allow God to reveal his divine power at work in our lives.

About one month prior to conception, the adult male produces thousands of spermatozoa (male germ cells) per second! Can you imagine how many are produced over one month's time? Each spermatozoon contains human DNA, but only one complete set of chromosomes. In other words, it's incomplete until it comes in contact with the female egg. Even though the male sperm *appears* to be a living organism, it's not considered alive because it can't reproduce a human life by itself! Also, out of the millions of spermatozoa that are formed, one...only one will actually fertilized the female egg for conception to actually take place.

So, how does this relate to our dreams? Ecclesiastes 5:7 states, "For in the multitude of dreams and many words there are also divers vanities: but fear thou God." Ideas, dreams, desires, visions come time and time again into our minds, just like those sperm cells generated by the male adult. There are so many sometimes, that it's frustrating for us to determine which ideas will actually come to pass.

As a matter of fact, many of the ideas lay dormant in our minds, or they may even race through our minds daily. They *appear* to be living organisms because many are indeed witty inventions, thoughts that have come from God and been inspired by the Holy Spirit. However, they're not alive because they can't reproduce by themselves. There is one dream, one purpose, one specific calling that God wants you to fulfill out of the plethora of ideas that have been formed. The only way for conception to take place is that it comes in contact with the female egg. With the spiritual eye, we'll call this your heart (Proverbs 16:1).

The conception of a dream happens when God reveals his purpose in man. God plants a seed on the inside of man, in his heart, and then the innate desire to become a purposeful being attaches to faith. Job 33:14-16 confirms that, "For God speaks once and twice his purpose for man, but man perceives it not. In a dream in a vision of the night, when deep sleep falls upon men, in slumbering upon the bed; then he opens the ears of men, and seals there instruction." Once the dream takes place it is our responsibility as believers to embrace what's been revealed by faith so that the process can began.

God definitely is not a respecter of persons, but indeed he is a respecter of faith. What determines a successful walk in Christ is when we settled it in within ourselves that we must walk by faith and not by sight. Many *hear* that statement, but not many have *heard* that statement. In other words many may hear but it doesn't actually register in their minds and their hearts, where action takes place. When we embrace God's method of operation we are sure to get supernatural results.

God always shows us the finished product before the process. I'll never forget a few years back I was invited to Milwaukee to minister at a birthday celebration. I was asked by the guest pastor to write a song for his wife and to sing it at the surprise celebration. I was so honored that before I got to Milwaukee I recorded the track and presented it to the Pastor's wife as a gift. Not really knowing that God was up to something and how he was really showing me a glimpse of what was to come.

The birthday celebration was a huge success and my mission was accomplished. The Pastor and wife were blessed by the gesture and invited me and my wife over to their home for dinner after church that Sunday. At the dinner table were renowned Pastors, Bishops along with their wives, and a renowned gospel artist. My wife and I were so honored to be in the mist of great people it was like we were in the presence of some of God's best generals. At the table the conversation was really good; we talked about marriage, ministry, and life in general. My wife and I were so impressed to hear their testimonies of how God had been faithful to them over the years, and then God started to expand our vision and show us a glimpse of what was to come.

Remember, God doesn't expose us to something if eventually we are not going to experience it. The Pastors started talking about properties that they were looking at in Florida that catered to families that owned private jets. My wife and I looked at each other as if to say, "We are just trying to maintain the home we have back in Michigan." My wife and I still laugh about this till this day. We share this story because God has a way of enlarging you where you are.

God will prepare you for what's to come before you even step into it, and when the thing becomes tangible and it comes into your possession you've already experienced it. When we experience the blessing before it is tangible, our instinct will always rely on God (The Blesser) because ultimately he is our source; therefore we will never put the blessing before the Blesser. You need to know that the dream that has been conceived on the inside of you is not impossible for you to obtain. Eph. 3:20 AMP says, "Now to him who by (in consequence of) the {action of His} power that is at work within us, is able to {carry out his purpose and} do superabundantly, far over and above all that we {dare} ask or think {infinitely beyond our highest prayers, desires, thoughts, hopes, or **DREAMS**}. You have to understand that this is just the beginning. Conception has taken place, however you still have to finish something. The dream at conception has ALREADY become reality – IT JUST NEEDS TO BE BORN!

Sometimes the dream that God gives us can be a bit overwhelming to say the least. Dreams can be intimidating, but with the dream God always reveals the provision. Dreams are ordained from God and it's up to you, the believer, to walk out the steps that God has ordained for you. Psalms 37:23 amplified states that, "the steps of a good man are directed and established by the Lord when he delights in his way and busies himself with his every step." The question is what are you doing to walk out the steps that God has ordained for you? Are you being consistent? Ultimately are you delighting yourself in the ways of the Lord? If you have come to the conclusion that one of the answers to these questions is no, then I have to be honest and say go back and walk out the steps.

Each step you take gets you closer to the ordained destination. A sporadic person can start anything, but it takes a consistent person to finish. It's amazing how thousands of churches and ministries start with amazing zeal and ambition. In fact, the call of God and the anointing is amazingly present as they begin, and all of a sudden life happens and they quit. Everybody asks the question what happen? The answer to that question is they quit because they missed a step trying to walk the entire mile first. You can't miss a step walking a mile as it relates to your dream. Every step you take is important, one step at a time. As you walk out the steps you get closer to where you're headed. Each step is very important because God wants to reveal something every step of the way bringing you to unlimited faith. Saints, the sky is no longer the limit to what you can have because in God there are no limits.

My wife and I were enjoying the weekend and Saturday night we decided to watch a little television to hear some good preaching. This particular Saturday night we were watching Pastor Bill Winston of Chicago Illinois and boy did God use that man to speak to me. It was like I was sitting in a chair by myself with no one around just me and him. He said and I quote, "Your potential is God"! I speak to you this day under the authority of the Holy Ghost that your potential is God! If God be for you He is more than the whole world against you.

What God has deposited into you is his full potential. God's potential cannot be measured and what you see in front of you is really a minor drop in the bucket in comparison to what God really can do. You are so close to finishing even if you just began.

Just endure. The dream was conceived in you because God knew that you could achieve it. 1 Corinthians 13:7 says, "Beareth all things, believeth all things, hopeth all things, endureth all things." Your hope is not in the dream alone, but it is in the One who loves you and ordained the dream. Keep moving and don't get complacent.

The world is waiting for the manifestation of the glory of God in your life.

The truth of the matter is you are the biggest giant that you will ever face. I know what you are saying right now. You're probably saying to yourself, "Man I needed to hear that". Can I be honest and say everyone needs to hear that eventually in their own life.

2 Timothy 1:7 says that God hasn't given us the spirit of fear but of power, love and a sound mind. Fear is indeed the opposite faith. Some of the ultimate fears in life are when the enemy can convince you that the word of God does not work, and or when the enemy can convince you to believe that you're incompetent concerning what God has conceived in you to do. A large sum of believers are literally walking in fear concerning what God told them because they don't believe they are capable of doing what God has said, or they're void of true understanding of what God has confirmed in His Word.

Fear only takes residence when faith is not present in the life of an individual. It is so important for a believer to keep himself in an environment of faith because it expels fear. It also causes the seed of faith to grow on the inside of you. Although dreams are given by God, they are conditional as it relates to coming to pass if you don't seek and believe God. As you seek God you must believe that he is and a rewarder to them who diligently seeks him.

As you get closer you will realize nothing else matters, and the supernatural ability that's on the inside of you will cause you to finish what God had started. Philippians 1:6 confirms, "I am convinced and sure of this very thing, that He who began a good work in you will continue until the day of Jesus Christ right up to the time of his return, developing that good work and perfecting and bringing it to full completion in you." The process of obtaining your dream can be quite a task. In fact you must understand in order to obtain it you must face obstacles to get to your ordained destination, or the place of victory.

You must understand as a believer that the trying of your faith can be the storm before the calm. James 1:2 NIV says, "Consider it pure joy, my brothers and sisters whenever you face trails of many kinds, because you know that the testing of your faith produces perseverance. Let perseverance finish its work so that you may be mature and complete, not lacking anything." Allow the ability of God to reveal your dream. Once you adhere to what he has revealed you will be fulfilled, healed, whole and at peace.

Life's circumstances were never designed to run us away from God, but to bring us closer to God. Never allow the enemy to cause you to trust in the world's way of stability. You must understand that your job and your investments is not your stability, but wisdom and knowledge is what makes you stable. Isaiah 33:6 says, "And He will be the security *and* stability of your times, a treasure of salvation, wisdom and knowledge; the fear of the Lord is your treasure." When you have the wisdom and knowledge you need to accomplish your God given dream, your focus will always be the fear and worshiping of the Lord. This will always be your connection to the thing he called you to.

Keep in mind, that whatever happens in the process of getting closer to the dream, your focus should be on God. God doesn't give you the desire to do something and not give you an open door. I speak momentum to your dream. I decree and declare you're walking into what God has promised and no weapon formed against you shall prosper. The weapon may form but it will not prosper. You're not going to die in the process, and that which was a failure to those in previous generations it will not be a failure to you. Keep moving don't place your tent in the middle of what slowed you down. Your steps are ordered by the Lord. Stay away from dead things. Hang around things that bring life.

Let me ask you a question as it relates to your Dream. How do you know your dream is from God? The answer is real simple. If the dream gives life, and life to others it is indeed from God. Anything opposite is death and it will bring death to other people. Jesus is the way the truth, and the life. God's plan before the foundation of this world was to awaken you toward your purpose, and to give you people and resources to connect you to your dream. II Peter 1:3 confirms that, "God has bestowed upon us all things that {are requisite and suited} to life and godliness, through the{ full, personal} knowledge of him who called us by and to his own glory and excellence (virtue)." As God's plan evolves for your life he will connect you to key people that can help you reach your dreams, and disconnect you from those that will deter you from your dream.

God's desire for your life is to radically change your world so that everything around you mirrors your purpose. Just let the Holy Spirit guide you to the ordained place. The Holy Spirit is our guide, our teacher, and comforter to lead us into all truth. The Holy Spirit is the best thing we can ever have as believers because we are guaranteed safety, comfort, and clarity toward direction we are headed in. The word of the Lord confirms that if we acknowledge him he will indeed direct our paths. Surely his goodness and his mercy shall follow us because God has paved the way already before the foundations of the world to get us to where we need to be. What God has purposed in you will be completed. You will finish it.

REFLECTION:

What is God saying to you about the conception of your dreams?

_____

_____

_____

_____

_____

_____

_____

_____

_____

_____

_____

_____

Chapter

2

You're Fail-Proof

GOD'S ORIGINAL PLAN and purpose still remains intact. Dominion was designed for man's assignment, and with God failure is never an option. God never fails! In fact, if anything seems like it's failed in your life understand this; you have God who lives in you and through you. It is not by your own power or your own might but by his spirit that you are held up in every area of your life. The word says lift up your eyes on high, and

17

behold who hath created these things, that bringeth out their host by number: he calleth them all by names by the greatness of his might, for that he is strong in power not one faileth. (Isaiah 40:26 KJV) God never fails and through him you'll never fail. Change your perception and watch God navigate you to your destined destination.

Your greatest influence in your life is your perception, and how you perceive will determine how you view your whole life. How you perceive God's Word will either propel you into something great or cause you to only go so far if you don't perceive God's Word correctly. Remember, your steps are ordered and God's plan for your life is to give you an expected end. When life happens understand it's not a failure issue it's a trust God issue. I want you to repeat very slowly with me the word issue. Are you ready? Let's do it. ISS –UE. Ok did you hear what you said? What you said was… If you heard it correctly you heard yourself say," It's you!"

Don't allow yourself to accept failure. It's not a part of your DNA. You were created in the image and likeness of God. You are a reflection of who he is. You are the workmanship of his hand. You are conduit that expresses the movement of God in the earth. Great is who you are, greatness is what's on the inside of you, and greater is where you are going. For the Bible declares that, "Ye are of God, little children, and have overcome them: because greater is he that is in you, than he that is in the world" (1 John 4:4).

I want to ask you a question. What would you do right now if you knew you couldn't fail? Think about it? Go back and reminisce about those failure moments, and recalculate everything you did. It's amazing how you come up with the right formula of what you should have done. When you acknowledge God the path you take will always be a lot clearer because he says" if you acknowledge me I will direct your path". God always provides revelation through whatever he promises. As he always confirms through his word that his word is a lamp unto our feet and a light unto our pathway. (Psalms 119:105)

God's plan is beyond what you can ever imagine. God in his sovereignty allows circumstances to happen in our lives to prove us and shows us how much we are nothing without him. He wants all the glory. When failure happens it can be embarrassing, but you don't have to stay there. God always orchestrates things with you in mind. You have to understand he is working on your behalf, and it is working for your good. Understand whatever you lost God can still restore. You may have failed as a business person, as a parent, as a friend, as an employee, as a spouse, or whatever role you play in life.... **THAT'S NOT THE SUM OF WHO YOU ARE!**

The enemy's desire is to keep you stuck looking at the image of failure. The enemy's desire is to see you fail because he failed. He's like that faithless person you know on your job that loves being miserable with people. You have to understand that his assignment on earth is to kill, still, and destroy every aspect of your faith. He can't kill you physically, but if he kills your faith everything unravels, and the ultimate outcome is death. You don't have time to yield to his way. God has invested so much in you, and he is looking for his return. The return is God himself.

The glory of God permeates through you like a treasure. 2 Corinthians 4:7 says, "However, we possess this precious treasure {the divine Light of the Gospel} in {frail, human} vessels of earth, that the grandeur and exceeding greatness of the power may be shown to be from God and not from ourselves". You must understand, and realize what you possess. I am often reminded of life circumstances that I've had to face. I've realized in moments I felt defeat that I had to remind myself that I possess something greater than me, greater than my own intellect, greater than my own opinion, greater than my own ability.

The fact of the matter is I cannot in my own strength face my issue. I would fall on my face every time. You cannot compare the authority that God has vs what the enemy has. There isn't any comparison. If we were to give any credit to the enemy the only authority that the enemy has is an amplified name over your situation. I am sure you are wondering what I am referring to? Well, let me bring more clarity to what I am trying to show you.

You see, the world we live in, is governed by names. Everything you have in this earthly realm that exists has a name. Jesus name is above every name on earth, and in heaven. So when you've been given a doctor report that says ...CANCER! Remember Jesus name is above that. DIVORCE! His name is above that. JOBLOSS! His name is better than that! REJECTION! His name is greater than that! You possess the greater, and Jesus has the ability to keep you from failing.

Perception is everything, and how you perceive God's word will either help you or defeat you. The scripture teaches that blessed are your eyes for they see. You have to see right in every circumstance. It's in that you will see that in God's word there is success. However, in the presence of God there is no failure. Don't let the spirit of religion keep you in perception of failure. Who told you that it was always going to be like this? Who told you that you have to remain where you are? Neither God nor his word! You have to settle in your heart that

God has a plan for you, and although the process seems long it has an end date.

True faith says that even if God doesn't do it, it doesn't mean he is not able. You have to trust God even if it hurts, and worship him no matter what. Can you lift your hands in the midst of what you thought was a failure? It's in that you will recognize that on the other side of your disappointment there is someone else on the other side that is screaming "YOU GOT THIS! I AM A TESTAMENT THAT YOU CAN MAKE IT"!

You must realize that the hand of God is upon your life and no matter what he is still God. He reigns over everything, and you reign with him in heavenly places. To really grasp and understand that you are fail proof you have to receive that statement by faith. The moment you think it's by your own intellect, strength, and ability that's the moment you will fall on your own face. You are fail proof because the power and treasure within is not of you. It is the supernatural ability of God that permeates through you. All glory belongs to him.

However, when we submit to the will of God we will find ourselves doing things, and operating at a supernatural level in every area of our life. God confirms throughout his word that we are fail proof when storms rage in our life. When all else fails your marriage will stand, your finances will stand, your health will remain, your family will stay intact, your life will never be the same. Hebrews 11:1 (Amplified) says, "Now faith is the assurance (the confirmation, the title deed) of things we hope for, being the proof of things we do not see and the conviction of their reality faith perceiving as real fact what is not revealed to the senses."

The mystery regarding God's word and what you see in the natural doesn't negate what God's Word says. When it seems impossible God's word says - it's possible. My friend, nothing can stop you from walking this thing out. Even if what you see doesn't show progress it doesn't mean you're lacking faith. There is nothing wrong with you. You remain consistent, and God's job is to bring forth the complete work. Sometimes you have to have your own pep rally. Declare the ending because you win!

God has equipped you for such a time as this, to go beyond what was established before you. What was placed before you was simply a platform that was built to take you higher. God knew generations before you would not have the ability to go any further. So, you were chosen to finish the course.

It is amazing how much we disqualify ourselves before we even take the first step. Sometime we compare ourselves to others not really realizing that what God has placed in us is special and unique. If we were all the same there would not be any need for any of us. We are all soldiers ordained to complete a mission. However, we all have different assignments. God has equipped us with a special ability to complete an assignment that can only be completed through you. The world is waiting for you to display what God has empowered you to complete. They are looking for something genuine, extraordinary, and authentic - someone like you. Are you ready?

REFLECTION:

What is God saying to you about being "Fail-Proof"?

_____

_____

_____

_____

_____

_____

_____

_____

_____

_____

_____

_____

_____

_____

Chapter

3

Your Plan & Blue Print

You carry the same last name. You have similar features. However, you are not the same in comparison to those you are related to. Thank God for where you came from, and appreciate your natural family heritage. That's definitely something worth being proud of. However, understand God called you. You are unique, and you cannot compare yourself with others you cannot be distracted with what others are doing. You have an assignment. Stay focused on the big picture.

Ephesians 3:19 says, "To know the love of Christ which passes knowledge; that you may be filled with all the fullness of God." In other words, your measure compared to somebody else does not determine your worth! The path that God has laid out for you can only be walked out by you. You can't be looking at other people that can be a major distraction. You can be so occupied by other people in what they are doing you can find yourself stagnated. You could find yourself not going any further than what you see.

God's Plan for you is far beyond what you see. I can recall living on the Westside of Detroit where I was born and raised and seeing a lot of suggestions. As a young man I wanted to be what I saw because it was my environment. Yes, I had dreams and ambitions but there were moments where I began to drift away. What I saw before me became my focus. I saw the gangs, and the glory of the street life, and it almost caused me to fall prey to things that could've changed the course of my life.

Growing up, being the only child, I was attracted to being accepted by the in crowd. Those that I was around were cool, they dressed a certain way, and the girls liked them. They were tough, and they knew how to take care of business if something went down. Being alone often, I found myself having to fight my own battles. I didn't have back up so I had to deal with bullying, and being picked on.

One particular day, I recall my neighbor started harassing me. I was targeted a lot because I was short, slightly overweight, and different. My mother, being a single parent, had to go to school and deal with a lot things because I was constantly in trouble. I was crying out to be accepted. My neighbor started teasing me for no reason, and I got extremely angry. Living in the city I had to learn to stand my ground, and deal with what was confronting me. The problem wasn't confronting the person, but it was how I confronted the person. I stormed into my house and I yelled, "Momma where is your gun? I am about to shoot him!" Thankfully I didn't get the gun. My mother wasn't having it. She wasn't going to allow her son to fall prey to the devil. However, this was the way of the streets, and the people I hung around glorified this way of life.

Sometimes we gravitate to what others are doing not knowing that we can take on the same exact struggles and mistakes if we try to be the same carbon copy. If that plan is not for you, then you can get stuck in someone else's plan. Ultimately, you could find yourself open to things like disappointment, pain and the demise of something great that God put in you. Then you may never have the opportunity to operate in your purpose.

When you are on the right path that God has for you, no matter what happens there is a focus to do what God is calling you to do. That determination will keep you on the ordained path. The steps of a righteous man, or right standing man, are ordered by the Lord. God will take you into places where you thought you couldn't imagine yourself to be.

The Scripture says, "Thus says the Lord who formed it to establish it (the Lord is His Name): 'Call to me, and I will answer you, and show you great and mighty things, which you do not know.'(Jeremiah 33:2-3 NKJV). I want you to understand that faith was designed to help us trust his purpose, and plan not to work our own will and plan. You may say in the season you are in right now, "I am not sure about this plan". You may be speaking to yourself saying, "What's the plan that God has for my life"? Trust in the Lord with all thine heart and lean not to your own understanding acknowledge him and he will direct your path. (Proverbs 3:16) When we trust God the plan is then revealed. Everything we thought wasn't clear becomes a reality, and before you know it, what is revealed causes you to walk out the plan.

Can you see the plan? Is it clear enough to walk out your steps? Do you see the blueprint? Keep trusting in God. Keep making the confession that your steps are ordered. No matter what you see in the natural, God has an expected end, just stay the course. What you see is subject to change, and God is empowering you to finish. He is restoring you and reviving you with his mighty hand. You are not stuck, you are moving forward, and the grace of God is holding your hand. You have the ability to perform this task. Stay in the environment of faith and stay connected to those that are moving forward in the things of God. However, through the process of walking your ordained path, God's word has to be in clear view, and taking root in your heart.

God's word is conceived in your heart, then formed by the tongue, and spoken out of your own mouth. It becomes a spiritual force releasing the ability of God within you. There is a path but you need his ability to complete it. Phil 4:13 says, "I can do all things through Christ that strengthens me. What happened here wasn't Paul's ability that made him say that, but the ability of God formed in him by the word, and out of the abundance of his heart the mouth spoke. You cannot complete the plan of God by yourself, but through Christ anything is possible. Your life is in his hands, and he has anointed you to finish.

The good thing about a plan is that it is always formulated by a thought, and then a blueprint generally is established. Once the blueprint is established, what's on paper is eventually constructed to become alive, and become a thriving entity. God knew his ultimate plan for you was to become something great. In fact, he saw something in you so precious that would bring him glory. He admired, was careful, and reverenced what he created. Psalms 139:14 affirms and articulates what God wants us all to know without a shadow of doubt. David says it like this, "That we are fearfully and wonderfully made, marvelous is thy works and our soul knows right well." You must understand that this is the blueprint of who you are. You are fearfully and wonderfully made and crafted by a masterful hand. You were fashioned by the hand of God, and by his workmanship you are a living blueprint of his divine plan.

The awesome thing about it is that your ultimate example is Jesus, and through the scriptures, we can mirror his life and achieve the same results. WOW! Can't you see that your life is outlined to win, succeed, accomplish, prosper, and fight against anything that will try to stop you from finishing? YOU ARE ANOINTED TO FINISH! I don't care what it looks like or how it feels, God has equipped you with something special to get the job done.

When life happens, recognize you don't have to figure it out on your own. Don't let what you've encountered be your portion. Yes, it may have hit you hard. Yes, maybe some things may not be functioning right. Remember you can always return to the original blueprint - just like a car. When something isn't working properly on your car you can't take it to a dealer or mechanic that doesn't understand how the car works. Why would you take a Jaguar to a Toyota dealer? You can't do that. It's not because they aren't able to work on other cars. It's because they aren't certified to work on that particular car. They don't understand the blueprint. You cannot go to everyone to get clarity, however when all else fails you can rest assure that the Word of God is the original blueprint to bring the answers you need.

If you don't understand the blueprint, always remember you can ask God. He will freely give you the understanding, clarity, wisdom, and ultimately the revelation needed to empower you to see things more clearly. James 1:5 (NIV) says, "If any of you lacks wisdom, you should ask God, who gives generously to all without finding fault, and it will be given to you". We must recognize that the plan of God is to never lead us astray, but to keep us on the right pathway. We must rely on him to be our source of direction.

You must recognize that they're a lot of sources in the world we live in, but there is only one true source, and that is Jesus who is the total fulfillment of all things. This journey was never designed for you to travel alone. God's plan was to walk with you every step of the way. Don't let the pressures of life's challenges cause you to be depressed. The moment the pressure comes cast your cares to the Father because he cares for you. Jesus said my yoke is easy and my burdens are light.

You aren't designed to carry this, so give it to Jesus. Rest in knowing that God's hand is upon your life, and if he is before you he is more than the whole world against you. Just continue to say yes, and God will perform through you like never before. What if you realized you can't lose? What's holding you from your next step of achieving? Do you really trust God? Don't allow the naysayers of unbelief to contaminate your faith. Be encouraged. Think it not strange when things try to come against the plan God has for you, it's a clear sign you are on target.

Nothing comes easy, but the blueprint was designed to navigate you through abrupt circumstances.

God never creates something and allows it to malfunction. His plan always overrides the turbulence of life. Listen to the voice of God when those moments happen because he wants to assure you and everyone that is connected, it is already done. Satan is already defeated and at the end of the story we win. Sometimes experiencing lost can slow you down. It can cause a serious blow to your faith. However, what makes a champion is not how many wins you have. It's the ability to get up with resolve after experiencing defeat and go for the win again. It's in that moment winning will be you portion.

REFLECTION:

What is God saying to you about your plan and blueprint?

_____

_____

_____

_____

_____

_____

_____

_____

_____

_____

_____

_____

_____

_____

Chapter

4

GETTING PAST THE
BATTLE IN YOUR MIND

THE BRAIN IS the most powerful organ that you have in your body, it can compute just like a computer and in some instances much faster. We must recognize and understand that although the brain is one of the most important organs in our body, guarding it is just as important. It's the place where thoughts are conceived. We must understand that the enemy's warfare tactics are extremely intentional toward it. If he can take over our thought patterns with his wicked suggestions, it can cause us to be stagnant in our faith.

It is imperative to understand that whatever is feeding you is what's leading you. The Bible teaches us to let this mind be in you which is also in Christ Jesus. The fact of the matter is, your thinking by itself is totally opposite in comparison to the mind of God. David explains it like this, "Such knowledge is too lofty to obtain marvelous is thy works and my soul knows right well." (Psalm 139:6) In other words, God's knowledge is so perfect. The way God thinks is far above measure in comparison to how man thinks. However, when we yield wholly toward his way God's mind takes precedence in our lives.

Not only do our thoughts need to be submitted to the will of God, but our decisions also. The fight is bigger than you. We wrestle against things that are not human. Ephesians KJV 6:12 says, "For we wrestle not against flesh and blood, but against principalities, against powers, against the rulers of the darkness of this world, against spiritual wickedness in high places."

I can recall when my father passed away and it was a traumatic time for our family. It was so painful that it was unreal. The effect was so subtle that it caused me not to even see what was attacking me. My will, my emotions, my physical body was under serious attack and I didn't realize that I was grieving which almost lead to severe depression. It didn't dawn on me until I went to my doctor. He asked me if I ever battled depression. It was then in that moment I heard Holy Spirit say, "No you have been grieving".

Through that it was revealed to me why my body was feeling the way it was feeling. I ate sporadically even when I wasn't hungry. I had different mood swings and I responded to people abruptly, even with my own family. However, my grieving wasn't without hope. 1 Thessalonians 4:13 says, "Brothers and sisters, we do not want you to be uninformed about those who sleep in death, so that you do not grieve like the rest of mankind, who have no hope" (NIV).

What I was dealing with left a door for the enemy to creep in with suggestions of depression that could've left me in a place of a demonic mental whirlwind. I recognized that I was broken in some major areas of my life that was causing me to be wounded naturally, and spiritually. God wanted to remind me that although this had happen in my life I am still anointed to finish because he was still with me.

The enemy has his shrewd methods, but God is smarter. He knows how to maneuver you out of places where you are stuck, to get you to the finish line of his ordained plan for your life. Don't stay there in defeat, and don't get comfortable when life happens. Move forward with everything you've got - stay focused. In Matthew 11:28-30 (NIV), Jesus said, "Come to me, all you who are weary and burdened, and I will give you rest. Take my yoke upon you and learn from me, for I am gentle and humble in heart, and you will find rest for your souls. For my yoke is easy and my burden is light." You must understand you cannot carry this on your own.

Altogether, when a challenge comes look to Jesus who is your help. He is standing and waiting on your beckoning call. Don't try to suppress those thoughts with random activity. Being active doesn't solidify true change. You must be consistently intentional with combating thoughts that keep you stagnate. Feed your thoughts with God's word and Godly suggestions that will feed your faith, and empower you to think on things above the turbulence of life. This battle is not yours it is the Lords.

REFLECTION:

What is God saying to you about how to get past the battle in your mind?

_____

_____

_____

_____

_____

_____

_____

_____

_____

_____

_____

_____

_____

_____

Chapter

5

CHANGE HAS COME!

I BELIEVE THAT a crisis never breaks the one who totally relies on God. No man can stand against the elements of this world by themselves. There is indeed a brighter day on the other side of the storm and when you come out on the other side it will definitely look like as though you have never been through anything. Isaiah 43:2 (NIV) says, "When you pass through the waters, I will be with you; and when you pass through the rivers, they will not sweep over you. When you walk through the fire, you will not be burned; the flames will not set you ablaze." You must understand the purpose of the crisis in a believer's life. It is a tool to transform you into the place of victory, nothing more and nothing less.

In the middle of your crisis you will learn how to rely on God more than you ever had in your entire life. You will recognize that you were never losing in the sense of losing, but you were gaining momentum to finish the course. Lay aside every weight and sin that so easily beset us, and let us run with patience the race that was set before us (Hebrews 12:1 KJV). God never allows something to leave your life and not give you more for your shame. Your change has come!

You will never be the same, going from glory to glory and from strength to strength. Your change had to come from the inside out in order to see the true ability that God has placed in you. The pressure you experienced was worth it. Fresh oil was crushed out of you to empower your steps to finish. Your resolve was recharged to not allow you to settle for what was stopping you.

Change is the new jersey you wear every day. It's a display of God's goodness, and favor toward you, and whatever you put your hands to do it's going to prosper. The aroma of change that appears in your life decontaminates the wiles of the devil. Every time he tries to remind you of your past - remind him of his future. Always remember to testify about what God did to display the change in your life. The people around you need to hear not only the story, but also the process of the story. It's in the testimony that precise answers will bring wholeness and assurance in someone else's life.

Always remember that God never just changes you for you; but ultimately for someone else, to hear what took place in your life when you encountered him. The change you have experience will cause your posture to change. You have a keen sense of spiritual discernment. You are on a pathway to blazing a trail that will affect generations. The way you speak is different. You are in a place where God is funneling new revelation daily to give you vision that will push you toward your end result.

You've been praying for this moment and it feels like you are so close. Every step you take is seems much easier, and you can hear in your spirit, "Keep Going, Press Your Way!" The worse part of your journey is just about over. You just have to keep moving forward because there is something greater on the other side. God Himself is rejoicing over you with singing (Zeph. 3:17). You are the trophy that God has on his mantle, and the glory of victory is on your life! Change has come and nothing, by any means, will stop your progress. You – yes you - are an unstoppable force!

REFLECTION:

What is God saying to you about how your change has come?

_____

_____

_____

_____

_____

_____

_____

_____

_____

_____

_____

_____

_____

Chapter
6

The Unction to Function

The world's view on a man's value is generally tied to his work. However, I believe it is tied to his anointing. You see you cannot allow yourself to be stagnated in envy in regards to what another man is doing. Ecclesiastes 4:4 says, "And I saw that all toil and all achievement spring from one person's envy of another. This too is meaningless, a chasing after the wind." You are unique, and what's on your life is an unction from the holy one and you know all things. There is no need to compare because you have been equipped to do something only God initiated you to do. It is through your hands only that it can be done. It's in God's sovereign plan that you will finish because he has empowered you to. You are the chosen vessel that will cause generations to be inspired.

I think about the first of many things God allowed me to do and yet he still never ceases to amaze me regarding the things he continues to do. I am grateful to be one of the first in my family to obtain a college degree. I was also one of the first in my family to maintain a marriage, and one of the first to accomplish things that I was never encouraged to do. I realized when I embraced the truth regarding my destiny; that I am free from the dysfunctional cycle of generational issues and it started wholeheartedly with me. I decided that I would be the first of first, and bring God glory to share my testimony of his goodness and grace toward me.

I came to the conclusion that I belong here. This statement speaks to the God given inheritance that belongs to me. I belong in the place of success. I belong in the place of victory. I belong in the place of abundance. I belong in the place of wholeness. This is what God has ordained for everyone that believes. You see your anointing comes from God to remove burdens and destroy yokes. Your life is the product of what an obedient vessel looks like when it yields to the will of God. The scripture says, "But you belong. The Holy One anointed you, and you all know it. I haven't been writing this to tell you something you don't know, but to confirm truth you do know, and to remind you that the truth doesn't breed lies" (1 John 2:20-21 MSG). Some of us have been lied to by individuals who were so comfortable in their misery that they wanted to paralyze you with a false sense of hope.

They told you lies because they didn't want you to believe what was true. They didn't want you to be first because they were comfortable with never being able to accomplish anything. 2 Corinthians 2:14 states, "But thanks be to God who always causes us to triumph in his name." This is your confirmation, your statement that cancels out everything that was formed to stop your progress in him. You are an agent of victory and you always triumph in his name.

I encourage you to keep before you those victories that you have won and use it as a reminder that no matter what, you always triumph. Yet and still through your most difficult times you are still standing. I tell you without any restraint that you have something special on your life. Those moments of pressure in your life was designed to bring the valued oil out of your life. The oil was pressed out of you as a symbol to empower you for the greater. Your wounds, scars, and pain were formed to give you an advantage.

What you experienced was necessary for the journey, and you will never be the same again. You cried your last tear of defeat, you have pressed and broke through to the other side. God has equipped you with faith that you will hold on to no matter the struggle. You have the unction to function. Say this and let it flow out of your spirit. "I am anointed. I am the healed. I am saved. I am prosperous. My family is blessed. I am victorious. I am more than a conquer, I have faith, and I believe God!" Don't allow the enemy to tell you something different. Keep it moving, and let those daily confessions cause you to be built up in your most holy faith towards your goals.

There is so much more on the inside of you. The enemy knows how great you are, and you are more powerful than you will ever know. The day you discover it, the enemy will fear you. As long as you ignore your God given potential, you are not a threat to the kingdom of darkness. However, once you get a revelation about your God given potential it will cause a revolution to take place in your life. The world is waiting to see you operate and see the display of God break forth in your life. Please recognize that the anointing on your life is ultimately for someone else to see. You are the specialist who has come out of hiding. You have a supernatural ability that causes you to do supernatural things. You are marked for this moment to do great exploits.

You are relevant for this time, and many will not understand. You are of great value for this Kingdom assignment, and you are equipped with the best of the best. This unction didn't come cheap, and now is the time. The word of the Lord is speaking to you, "Not by power, not by might but by his spirit" (Zech. 4:6). God has called you with a holy calling and he is with you. It's the new normal, so get used to greater.

REFLECTION:

What is God saying to you about your unction to function?

_____

_____

_____

_____

_____

_____

_____

_____

_____

_____

_____

_____

_____

Chapter

7

THE ULTIMATE GOAL

PROGRESS MEANS YOU are moving toward a goal, but that *doesn't* mean you are not absent from abrupt things that slow you down. That's not an indication that you should stop or make you feel as though it can't be done. It just means you cannot do this on your own strength. You should rest in knowing that the longer you wait the greater the anointing, and strength to finish. Don't faint, don't get frustrated - just stay the course. You have to recognize the purpose of a challenge. The challenge will manifest while you're on the journey of finishing making you aware that it's not your ability, but God's ability. Through his ability we recognize that we can do all things through Christ that enables us to finish; because he is the true source of our strength.

When your ultimate goal is to finish something bigger than you, you will experience an unusual press. The press is to squeeze the potential, value, ultimately the best out of you. It's in moments like these you really notice the greater one working through you, maximizing the potential in you. Just like the process of the olive and getting the precious oil to be used, you represent the olive, and the oil represents the anointing. In order for the oil to flow, you - the olive, must be crushed. Everything that has challenged you from the start of this journey is a representation of the crushing process. The crushing process is the direct personal issue that provoked the growth in you: the crush of disappointments, the crush of things that challenge your character, the crush of failures, the crush of heartache, the crush of rejection. This is really the beginning of something new, and you must recognize that God has our best interest at heart.

There were many times in my life where I felt the pressure of being crushed, but it was in that I experienced the power of the anointed one permeating through my life. It was an empowerment to propel me to another victory. God's way of doing things can definitely be challenging at times, but know his plan is the best plan for your life. While moving in the direction toward the ultimate goal you must abide and focus on the word of God. If you give place to the enemy while you're on the last leg of the journey to finish, you can experience unplanned delays that slow you down. There can be delays of foolishness, delays of sin, and delays of shame.

I was at work one day and a man came into our facility to ask about our program. Midway through the conversation he asks me, "Do you go to church?" I said, "Yes." He continued, "What church do you attend?" I answered, "World Changers in Detroit." After a brief stint of conversation, I gave him the directions to the church. He shakes my hand, and I said, "God bless you brother." He paused with tears in his eyes and said, "Sir, thank you for the information. Can I share a small proverb with you?" I said, "Sure!" He said, "My father use to tell me, 'Son, if you see a detour sign in life keep straight.'" He said, "To be honest - I saw that detour sign and ran right into it. I just need to get on track." Then he walked away.

I share this to you tell you that the enemy will place roadblocks to detour you from getting to where you need to be. Make the choice not to run into the illusion of another pathway. Proverbs 14:12 (NIV) says, "There is a way that appears right, but in the end it leads to death." Keep straight because you are on target to finish something big. The word of the Lord says, "He who looks carefully into the perfect law the law of liberty, and faithfully abides by it, not having become a {careless} listener who forgets but an active doer{who obeys}, he will be blessed and favored by God in what he does {in his life of obedience}" (James 1:25 AMP). You are blessed, you are victorious, and you can settle it in your spirit even now nothing by any means should stop you from moving toward the greater. God's mighty hand is pushing you forward. There's no stopping you now my sister and brother, you are on the move toward your ultimate goal.

REFLECTION:

What is God saying to you about achieving your ultimate goal?

_____

_____

_____

_____

_____

_____

_____

_____

_____

_____

_____

_____

_____

Chapter

8

MOVING FORWARD IN A PANDEMIC

WHO WOULD'VE THOUGHT in this lifetime that we would have experienced a pandemic that would change the normalcy of how we do everyday life. Covid-19 will be engraved in our country's history for generations to come. One day we were doing things that were a part of our everyday life. We were at school, work, the mall, sports events, visiting loved ones, at church, at conferences, eating in restaurants, traveling to different cities. Then everything literally stopped in its tracks. The plans that we prepared for tomorrow literally swallowed up by the inevitable and everything came to an abrupt stop.

It didn't matter where you were financially everyone was affected. People all over the world were brought to a halt. Hospitals were packed to capacity and the healthcare system was on overload. It seemed as though there was nothing we could do, but it was in that moment God began to shine the pathway toward what mattered the most.

Our home was attacked and my wife and I contracted the Covid-19 virus. After traveling south for a conference we had to be quarantined for about 30 days. We weren't sure if the virus was contracted through traveling, but we do know we went through something that changed our whole perspective on life. Thankfully and moderately we came out on the other side of this invisible enemy. We were victorious. However, we knew many individuals, both far and near, that didn't make it.

It was because of this we had an internal determination to witness and testify of the goodness of the Lord.

Psalms 19:7-14 KJV says, "The law of the Lord is perfect, converting the soul: the testimony of the Lord is sure, making wise the simple." God allows things to happen in our life to bring out the better in us that will ultimately bring him glory for the world to see his goodness.

You see, many things took place, and we had many plans that we planned for, but God had better plans. He wanted to teach us, and guide us how to move forward in a pandemic. He shut down the world's systems and resources so he could show us that He is ultimate resource for our lives. He wanted our attention, and we were able to focus our attention on God while building our faith and family. So, what the enemy meant for bad, God turned this around for our good. God made a huge statement in the earth that was empowered by his fierce love and he said, "Return to Me"! Hosea 6:1, says "COME AND let us return to the

Lord, for He has torn so that He may heal us; He has stricken so that He may bind us up."

God allowed this to take place in our life. This was a crisis designed to equip us, and not to harm us. The word of the Lord says, "We shall live and not die and declare the works of the Lord" (Psalms 118:17 KJV). This was and prayer and confession of our faith during the situation at hand. There are moments in our lives that we can forget what's really important. We must recognize that we cannot do things on our own strength. God is the source of our accomplishments and achievements.

Moving forward in any circumstance is easy when we know he is indeed with us. God is the source of our hope, and that hope is the expectation of what is good in our lives. Romans 15:13 (NLT) says, "I pray that God, the source of hope, will fill you completely with joy and peace because you trust in him. Then you will overflow with confident hope through the power of the Holy Spirit." It is through circumstances of life we should focus on eternal things because ultimately that's what matters the most in times like these.

As my wife and I went through this season the enemy really attacked our thoughts, our bodies, and it really shook our faith. I remember the same day I was diagnosed with Covid-19 and how numb I felt. Mentally my mind was racing with so many questions. Fear and anxiety was literally trying to invade my space. The nurse advised me medically to stay home and quarantine for at least 7-14 days. I recognized then I was in a spiritual battle. This sickness was a huge distraction to divert me to a place of defeat. The enemy was literally trying to keep me in a place of stagnation. This battle continued to intensify to the next level.

That same exact week we were bombarded with the news of loved ones passing away, after talking to them just days before they had contracted the virus. To add to the pressure, my wife, in the midst of taking care of me, was rushed to the hospital due to shortness of breath; later to find out she had Covid-19 as well. Here we both were, sick and heartbroken at the same time. Thankfully our children were not affected physically, but emotionally, it was hard to see their parents in this state while grieving other loved ones at the same time. How do you process all of this in one week? How do you adjust when circumstances are feeling like a title wave and a Mack truck has hit, all at the same time?

Emotionally, you are a wreck but for some reason you have a spiritual resolve that brings you to a place of peace. Although you may not have been here before, you know without a doubt that the track record of God has been consistent in your life. In the midst of this pandemic trail, God spoke to us so clear. His love held us together in the midst of our brokenness. His hand of mercy and grace covered us like a shield. We never questioned God why, but he revealed to us everything will come together for the good of you both. We kept our focus, as we were checked on every day by our family, friends and pastors. Our sickness became a banner of victory, as we rested in our healing. Jesus was healing us and turning what happened to us into a testimony of his divine intervention.

Through it all we never wavered, but the challenge of what happened to us was real. We had to make daily confessions in spite of what our body was feeling. We declared the name of the Lord over our home; he became the banner over our home. Jehovah Nissi! The Lord our banner! His name alone causes change to happen suddenly. As we lay in our bed of affliction, we encountered him. Jesus had invaded our space. He spoke to us with a small voice, "This too shall pass and greater is coming." When you speak his name, not only do you acknowledge him he brings with him the effect of his name. In his name there is healing, restoration, salvation, joy, peace, power, deliverance, and prosperity. You must recognize everything you need is in the banner of Jehovah Nissi.

God was manifesting his glory through our lives, and through what we experienced a greater portion of the anointing was being placed on our lives. We recognized that everything that we've went through God was granting a greater grace to impart healing into someone else's life.

REFLECTION:

What did God say to you about moving forward during the pandemic?

_____

_____

_____

_____

_____

_____

_____

_____

_____

_____

_____

_____

_____

Chapter

9

The Ultimate Finisher

Throughout the scriptures Jesus always had the last word. Whether it was through profound parables he spoke or through his miracle working actions he had a way of finishing his divine assignment. He left nothing unturned. He was serious about his father's business even until his death on the cross. Although his track record spoke for itself, he still sealed what he had done with his own three words over 2,000 years ago saying, "It is finished"! Those three words still echo with power through the lives of every believer till this day. Miracles, signs and wonders are readily available to us because what was done on the cross.

As we look deeply at these three words, you must look at it from its Greek translation and the word meaning. The Greek word for the phrase "It is finished" is *tetelestai* which means to bring to an end, to complete, or to accomplish something successfully. This action word means more than that in its perfect tense. It means what Jesus did it happened, but what makes this word carry more weight is that it means it's still in effect today. Jesus is the ultimate finisher. His statement didn't mean he was finished. It was a statement to make an ever-lasting effect that victory belongs to Jesus. Nothing by any means can hold you from obtaining your blood bought right. You must recognize you have been victorious in your past, your present, and ultimately in your future. How so? I am glad you asked. You see it took your past to bring you to your future, and even if it was a rough past God didn't let you die in it. I think that's worth a praise!

Jesus is our great example it is through his eternal deeds we carrier the mantle of victory on our lives. Continue to build yourself up in your most holy faith in moments it feels like reaching your goal is impossible. Learn to celebrate each step. Rehearse your victory lap, and see yourself completing the journey. This journey of finishing is more than talk, it's faith in action. Whatever the task is at hand you can do it.

I recall many stories of personal victories, and I had to place before me the ultimate finisher. Jesus was my focus, and nothing was going to keep me from seeing the pathway he has set before me. How bad do you want it? Are you willing to press pass the illusions of defeat? I recall a story about a man who was pursuing an opportunity to become the next fire chief in our city. He had served as an excellent firefighter for over 25 years. However, for some reason he didn't qualify for the chief position. He kept applying, and praying in secret. Something on the inside of him caused him not to settle for that news. When you know that something belongs to you it doesn't matter how long it takes to get it. You are willing to wait and go through the challenge of it. He did the unthinkable. He purchased the chief uniform and everything with it. Every morning he got up before he left for work and tried on his uniform, looked in the mirror, and told himself, "Good morning chief, have a great day!" As crazy as that seemed, he decided in his secret place to embrace what belong to him. Eventually through his journey of becoming, he became what he believed – the chief.

Matthew 6:6 states, "But when you pray, go into your room, close the door and pray to your father who is unseen. Then your father, who sees what is done in secret will reward you openly." It's not a matter of when; it's about **what** you do before it happens. You can't allow the voice of distraction to talk you down from the high place of determination. Jesus proved through moments of distraction his response was the word of his power. Those results are evident in your life, and when you start again remember it's not by your power, strength, but by his spirit says the Lord.

Jesus is totally the undisputed champion of finishing. His record is flawless. Everything he was destined to do in this earth realm was completed even before the foundations of this world. He is the beginning and the end, The Alpha, and Omega, The First and the Last; yet direct in his approach. 1 John 3:8b AMPC says, "The reason the son of God was made manifest (visible) was to undo (destroy, loosen, and dissolve) the works of the devil{has done}". There is nothing that should hold you back from moving forward to your goal. Jesus destroyed all the works of the devil. Those works of sin, procrastination, limited thinking, generational curses, guilt, shame, and every device formed against you to finish. It has been annihilated by the hands of the ultimate finisher - Jesus Christ the Anointed One with the anointing. You are empowered to succeed because of what Jesus did. It's time to defy the odds. You are Anointed to Finish!

REFLECTION:

What is God saying to you about The Ultimate Finisher?

_____

_____

_____

_____

_____

_____

_____

_____

_____

_____

_____

_____

_____

_____

CPSIA information can be obtained
at www.ICGtesting.com
Printed in the USA
BVHW071622300421
606209BV00005B/549

9 781662 811098